Table of Contents

Introduction

In the early days of the web, anyone who wanted to build a web application had to own the physical hardware required to run a server, which is a cumbersome and expensive undertaking.Then came the cloud, where fixed numbers of servers or amounts of server space could be rented remotely. Developers and companies who rent these fixed units of server space generally over-purchase to ensure that a spike in traffic or activity wouldn't exceed their monthly limits and break their applications. This meant that much of the server space that was paid for usually went to waste. Cloud vendors have introduced auto-scaling models to address the issue, but even with auto-scaling an unwanted spike in activity, such as a DDoS attack, could end up being very expensive.Serverless is a cloud computing execution model where the cloud provider dynamically manages the allocation and provisioning of servers. A serverless application runs in stateless compute containers that are event-triggered, ephemeral (may last for one invocation), and fully managed by the cloud provider. Pricing is based on the number of executions rather than pre-purchased compute capacity.The code is typically run inside stateless containers that can be triggered by a variety of events including http requests, database events, queuing services, monitoring alerts, file uploads, scheduled events (cron jobs), etc. The code that is sent to the cloud provider for execution is usually in the form of a function. Hence serverless is sometimes referred to as "Functions as a Service" or "FaaS". Serverless applications are event-driven cloud-based systems where application development rely solely on a combination of third-party services, client-side logic and cloud-hosted remote procedure calls (Functions as a Service). As developer Mike Roberts explains, the term was once used for so-called back-end-as-a-service scenarios, where a mobile app would connect to a back-end server hosted entirely in the cloud. But today when people talk about serverless computing, or a serverless architecture, they mean function-as-a-service offerings, in which a customer writes code that only tackles business logic and uploads it to a provider. That provider takes care of all hardware provisioning, virtual machine and container management, and even tasks like multithreading that often are built into application code.The term "Serverless" is confusing since with such applications there are both server hardware and server processes running somewhere, but the difference compared to normal approaches is that the organization building and supporting a 'Serverless' application is not looking after that hardware or those processes. They are outsourcing this responsibility to someone else.

History of serverless computing

The term 'serverless' can be traced to its original meaning of not using servers and typically referred to peer-to-peer (P2P) software or client-side only solutions. In the cloud context, the current serverless landscape was introduced during an AWS re:Invent event in 2014. Since then, multiple cloud providers, industrial, and academic institutions have introduced their own serverless platforms.

Serverless seems to be the natural progression following recent advancements and adoption of VM and container technologies, where each step up the abstraction layers led to more lightweight units of computation in terms of resource consumption, cost, and speed of development and deployment. Furthermore, serverless builds upon long-running trends and advances in both distributed systems, publish-subscribe systems, and event-driven programming models,including actor models,reactive programming,and active database systems.Serverless platforms can be considered an evolution of Platform-as-a-Service (PaaS) as provided by platforms such as Cloud Foundry, Heroku, and Google App Engine (GAE). PaaS was defined by NISTe as "the capability provided to the consumer is to deploy onto the cloud infrastructure consumer-created or acquired applications created using programming languages and tools supported by the provider. The consumer does not manage or control the underlying cloud infrastructure including network, servers, operating systems, or storage, but has control over the deployed applications and possibly application hosting environment configurations." In this definition, users are expected to manage deployments of applications and have control over hosting environment configurations.Serverless FaaS, when compared to this definition of PaaS, is removing user control over hosting to provide simpler scaling and more attractive billing model: the cloud provider controls the hosting environment's configuration, runs user-provided code only when it is invoked, and only bills for actual usage while hiding the complexity of scaling (in practice implementing auto-scaling in PaaS is not easy and it is very difficult to scale to zero). That is a significant change when compared to the previous generation of PaaS (which could be considered first generation of PaaS) and it is very attractive for PaaS users that do not need to pay for idle resources and avoid managing auto-scaling rules.The main differentiators of serverless platforms is transparent autoscaling and fine-grained resource charging only when code is running. That should not to be confused with free-usage quota, where limited monthly resource quota is available, but counted even if the application is not used. For example, GAE Standard is priced in "instance hours"f and even if the app is not used the instance is kept running. Later, GAE added Flexible version with a more fine-grained billing unit, but still developers will be billed even if server is not used. That can lead to unexpected outcomes when the bill arrives at the end of month for forgotten test services.Mobile Backend as-a-Service (MBaaS) or more generalized Backend as-a-Service (BaaS) bears a close resemblance to serverless computing. Some of those services even provided "cloud functions" (for example, Facebook's now-defunct Parse Cloud Code). Such code, however, was typically limited to mobile use cases.Software-as-a-Service (SaaS) may support the server-side execution of user-provided functions, but they are executing in the context of an application and hence limited to the application domain. Some SaaS vendors allow the integration of arbitrary code hosted somewhere else and invoked via an API call. For example, this is approach is used by the Google Apps Marketplace in Google Apps for Work.The boundaries defining serverless computing functionality overlaps with PaaS and SaaS. One way to categorize serverless is to consider the varying levels of developer control over the infrastructure. In an IaaS model, the developer has much more control over the resources, but is responsible for managing both the application code and operating the infrastructure. This gives the developer great flexibility and the ability to customize every aspect of the application and infrastructure, such as administering VMs, managing capacity and utilization, sizing the workloads, achieving fault tolerance and high availability. PaaS abstracts away VMs and takes care of managing underlying operating systems and capacity, but the developer is responsible for the full life cycle of the code that is deployed and run by the platform, which does not scale down to zero. SaaS represent the other end of the spectrum where the developer has no control over the infrastructure, and instead get access to prepackaged components. The developer is allowed to host code there, though that code may be tightly coupled to the platform. BaaS is similiar to SaaS in that the functionality is targeting specific use cases and components, for example, MBaaS provide backend functionality needed for mobile development such as managing push notifications, and when it allows developer to run code it is within that backend functionality.

What is serverless?

That's where serverless computing comes into play. Serverless is an approach that aims to address infrastructure and software architecture issues I've outlined above by:

Using a managed compute service such as AWS Lambda, Azure Functions, Google Cloud Functions, IBM OpenWhisk, or Auth0 WebTask to execute code

Leveraging third-party services and APIs in a more thoughtful way

Applying serverless architectures and patterns.

Serverless is about streamlining the complexity of traditional systems by abolishing the need to run servers and manage infrastructure, and its' about helping developers focus on their core problem by reducing the amount of code they need to write. By taking a serverless compute service and making use of various powerful single-purpose APIs and web services, developers can build loosely coupled, scalable, and efficient architectures quickly. In this way, developers can move away from servers and infrastructure concerns, and focus primarily on code, which is the ultimate goal behind serverless.Let's unpack what this really means. A serverless compute service, such as AWS Lambda, can execute code in response to events in a massively parallel way. It can respond to HTTP requests (using the AWS API Gateway), events raised by other AWS services, or it can be invoked directly using an API. As with S3, there is no need to provision capacity for Lambda, writes Sam Kroonenburg. There are no servers to monitor or scale, there is no risk to cost by over-provisioning, and there's no risk to performance by under-provisioning (PDF document). Users are only charged for the time that their code executes, which is measured in seconds.A user never pays for any idling servers or unused capacity. This is fundamentally different from what developers have been used to doing. The unit of scale in serverless is an ephemeral function that runs only when needed. This leads to an interesting and noticeable outcome: the performance of code visibly and measurably affects its cost. The quicker the function stops executing, the cheaper it is to run. This can, in turn, influence the design of functions, approach to caching, and how many and which dependencies the function relies on to run much more than in traditional server-based systems.Serverless compute functions are typically considered to be stateless. That is, the state isn't kept between function instantiation. Developers must not assume that local resources and processes remain each time a function runs. "None of the in-process or host state that you create will be available to any subsequent invocation" (Roberts, 2016).Statelessness is powerful because it allows the platform to quickly scale to handle an ever-changing number of incoming events or requests. Having said that, the Lambda runtime does reuse its lightweight Linux containers, which run functions under the hood. Developers who copied files over to the container's filesystem (/tmp directory) or ran processes, might find them again on subsequent instantiations.This can be useful, but it can lead to additional work for the function if it has to clean up at the start or the end of each invocation. Nevertheless, Lambda does reserve the right to recreate containers at any time, so developers cannot rely on those files and processes being there. It's important to note that the term "serverless" has received a lot of pushback, as some people feel that it is misleading. Serverless refers to the fact that we, as users of these technologies, do not have access to the actual servers. Naturally, there are still servers running in the background, but we do not have any ability to access or manage them. Rather, it is the vendor, such as Amazon, Google, or Microsoft, that is in charge of the machines. The vendor is responsible for providing a highly-available compute infrastructure—including capacity provisioning and automated scaling.Some people argue that serverless should be referred to as function as a service (FaaS), and while it's not a bad name, serverless is a much broader concept than just an ephemeral function running in the cloud. But FaaS is a good term to use when referring specifically to services such as AWS Lambda, Google Cloud Functions, or Azure Functions.Serverless functions, or FaaS, are not just a platform as a service (PaaS) technology in disguise. The unit of scale between common PaaS systems and serverless functions is different. Traditional PaaS systems aren't as granular — you still have to work out the number of dynos or VMs to provision — and take a lot longer to provision and de-provision than do serverless systems.When a new serverless function needs to be created, it happens on the order of a few seconds for a cold function, and on the order of milliseconds for a warm function. The actual time it takes to spin up a cold function depends on several factors, such as the language runtime (Lambda supports JavaScript, Python and Java) and the number of dependencies you need to load.Serverless cloud technologies such as Lambda are built on containers, but the advantage for us is that we don't need to manage them. We can spend most of our time thinking about code and software architecture instead. It's the vendor who has to work out the most efficient way to allocate resources and computing capacity, not us.

Tim Wagner, GM of Lambda, referenced this in the keynote at the first conference on serverless technologies in New York, when he said that Lambda attempts to solve the world's largest bin packing problem. It's just as well that they have to do it and

What is serverless computing?

Serverless computing enables developers to build applications faster by eliminating the need for them to manage infrastructure. With serverless applications, the cloud service provider automatically provisions, scales, and manages the infrastructure required to run the code.In understanding the definition of serverless computing, it's important to note that servers are still running the code. The serverless name comes from the fact that the tasks associated with infrastructure provisioning and management are invisible to the developer. This approach enables developers to increase their focus on the business logic and deliver more value to the core of the business. Serverless computing helps teams increase their productivity and bring products to market faster, and it allows organizations to better optimize resources and stay focused on innovation.Serverless computing is an execution model for the cloud in which a cloud provider dynamically allocates—and then charges the user for—only the compute resources and storage needed to execute a particular piece of code. Naturally, there are still servers involved, but their provisioning and maintenance are entirely taken care of by the provider. This includes nothing that would be bare metal, nothing that's virtual, nothing that's a container—anything that involves you managing a host, patching a host, or dealing with anything on an operating system level, is not something you should have to do in the serverless world." As developer Mike Roberts explains, the term was once used for so-called back-end-as-a-service scenarios, where a mobile app would connect to a back-end server hosted entirely in the cloud. But today when people talk about serverless computing, or a serverless architecture, they mean function-as-a-service offerings, in which a customer writes code that only tackles business logic and uploads it to a provider. That provider takes care of all hardware provisioning, virtual machine and container management, and even tasks like multithreading that often are built into application code.Serverless functions are event-driven, meaning the code is invoked only when triggered by a request. The provider charges only for compute time used by that execution, rather than a flat monthly fee for maintaining a physical or virtual server. These functions can be connected together to create a processing pipeline, or they can serve as components of a larger application, interacting with other code running in containers or on conventional servers.Serverless computing can be defined by its nameless thinking (or caring) about servers. Developers do not need to worry about low-level details of servers management and scaling, and only pay for when processing requests or events. We define serverless as follows:

Serverless computing is a platform that hides server usage from developers and runs code on-demand automatically scaled and billed only for the time the code is running.

This definition captures the two key features of serverless computing:

Costbilled only for what is running (pay-as-you-go). As servers and their usage is not part of serverless computing model, then it is natural to pay only when code is running and not for idle servers. As execution time may be short, then it should be charged in fine-grained time units (like hundreds of milliseconds) and developers do not need to pay for overhead of servers creation or destructions (such as VM booting time). This cost model is very attractive to workloads that must run occasionally; serverless essentially supports "scaling to zero" and avoid need to pay for idle servers. The big challenge for cloud providers is the need to schedule and optimize cloud resources.

Elasticityscaling from zero to "infinity." Since developers do not have control over servers that run their code, nor do they know the number of servers their code runs on, decisions about scaling are left to cloud providers. Developers do not need to write auto-scaling policies or define how machine-level usage (CPU, memory, and so on) translates to application usage. Instead they depend on the cloud provider to automatically start more parallel executions when there is more demand for it. Developers also can assume the cloud provider will take care of maintenance, security updates, availability and reliability monitoring of servers.

Serverless computing today typically favors small, self-contained units of computation to make it easier to manage and scale in the cloud. A computation, which can be interrupted or restarted, cannot depend on the cloud platform to maintain its state. This inherently influences the serverless computing programming models. There is, however, no equivalent notion of scaling to zero when it comes to state, since a persistent storage layer is needed. However, even if the implementation of a stateful service requires persistent storage, a provider can offer a pay-as-you-go pricing model that would make state management serverless. We are seeing providers releasing services that stretch the definition of serverless, and the definition may evolve over time. For example, Amazon Aurora is a "serverless" database service, which supports powerful auto-scaling capabilities but requires minimum memory and CPU allocations and hence does not scale to zero and has ongoing costs.The most natural way to use serverless computing is to provide a piece of code (function) to be executed by the serverless computing platform. It leads to the rise of Function-as-a-service (FaaS) platforms focused on allowing small pieces of code represented as functions to run for limited amount of time (at most minutes), with executions triggered by events or HTTP requests (or other triggers), and not allowed to keep persistent state (as function may be restarted at any time). By limiting time of execution and not allowing functions to keep persistent state FaaS platforms can be easily maintained and scaled by service providers. Cloud providers can allocate servers to run code as needed and can stop servers after functions finish as they run for limited amount of time. If functions must maintain state, then they can use external services to persist their state.

FaaS is an embodiment of serverless computing principles, which we define as follows:

Function-as-a-Service is a serverless computing platform where the unit of computation is a function that is executed in response to triggers such as events or HTTP requests.

Our approach to defining serverless is consistent with emerging definitions of serverless from industry. For example, Cloud Native Computing Foundation (CNCF) defines serverless computing11 as "the concept of building and running applications that do not require server management. It describes a finer-grained deployment model where applications, bundled as one or more functions, are uploaded to a platform and then executed, scaled, and billed in response to the exact demand needed at the moment." While our definition is close to the CNCF definition, we make a distinction between serverless computing and providing functions as a unit of computation. As we discuss in the research challenges section, it is possible that serverless computing will expand to include additional aspects that go beyond today's relatively restrictive stateless functions into possibly long-running and stateful execution of larger compute units. However, today serverless and FaaS are often used interchangeably as they are close in meaning and FaaS is the most popular type of serverless computing.

Paul Johnston (co-founder of ServerlessDays) defined serverless as follows: "A serverless solution is one that costs you nothing to run if nobody is using it (excluding data storage)." This definition highlights the most important characteristic of serverless computingpays-as-you-go. It assumes serverless computing is a subset of cloud computing so auto-scaling is included and developers have no access to servers. CNCF and our definitions emphasize not only pay-as-you-go or "scale to zero" aspects, but also the lack of need to manage servers.

Another way to define serverless computing is by what functionality it enables. Such an approach emphasizes "serverless is really about the managed services" and FaaS can be treated as cloud "glue," as described by Steven Faulkner (a senior software engineer at LinkedIn). It is "glue" that joins applications composed of cloud services. Such a definition addresses only a narrow set of use cases where serverless computing is used, while our definition captures the important use cases, which we will highlight in the accompanying sidebars.

All definitions share the observation that the name 'serverless computing' does not mean servers are not used, but merely that developers can leave most operational concerns of managing servers and other resources, including provisioning, monitoring, maintenance, scalability, and fault-tolerance to the cloud provider.

Why Serverless

Serverless computing offers a number of advantages over traditional cloud-based or server-centric infrastructure. For many developers, serverless architectures offer greater scalability, more flexibility, and quicker time to release, all at a reduced cost. With serverless architectures, developers do not need to worry about purchasing, provisioning, and managing backend servers. However, serverless computing is not a magic bullet for all web application developers. Serverless computing can simplify the process of deploying code into production. Scaling, capacity planning and maintenance operations may be hidden from the developer or operator. Serverless code can be used in conjunction with code deployed in traditional styles, such as microservices. Alternatively, applications can be written to be purely serverless and use no provisioned servers at all.The difference between traditional cloud computing and serverless is that you, the customer who requires the computing, doesn't pay for underutilized resources. Instead of spinning up a server in AWS for example, you're just spinning up some code execution time. The serverless computing service takes your functions as input, performs logic, returns your output, and then shuts down. You are only billed for the resources used during the execution of those functions. Serverless architectures are internet-based systems where the application development does not use the usual server process.

Instead, they rely solely on a combination of third-party services, client-side logic and service-hosted remote procedure calls (Functions as a Service)."Not the usual server process" means that your software isn't running on a server that you have access to. You don't own those servers. You can't log in to them, even if you wanted to. They are abstracted away and managed for you by someone else, typically a cloud provider.

There are many immediate benefits to not managing your own servers:

You don't have to worry about them randomly rebooting or going down.

You don't end up with snowflake servers, where you don't know quite what's installed on them but they are mission-critical to your organisation.

You're not responsible for installing software on them. Even if you use configuration management tools such as Chef or Ansible to automate this, that's still extra code you have to maintain over time.

The value of serverless computing

Serverless computing enables operational simplicity by removing the need for infrastructure setup, configuration, provisioning and management. Serverless computing architectures require less overhead compared to those in which developers target the virtual machines (VMs) or containers directly.Infrastructure is automated and elastic in serverless computing, which makes it particularly appealing for unpredictable workloads, not to mention more cost-efficient. Most importantly, serverless architectures enable developers to focus on what they should be doing — writing code and optimizing application design — making way for business agility and digital experimentation.The benefits of serverless computing must be balanced against its drawbacks, including vendor-lock in, inevitable skills gaps and other architectural limitations.

Key capabilities of serverless computing

At its foundational level, serverless functions eliminate the need for end users to manually manage the infrastructure. In turn, it provides these key capabilities:

Runs code residing as functions without the need for the user to explicitly provision or manage infrastructure such as servers, VMs and containers

Automatically provisions and scales the runtime environment, including all the necessary underlying resources (specifically the compute, storage, networking and language execution environment) required to execute many concurrent function instances

Offers additional capabilities for test and development environments along with service assurance purposes, such as monitoring, logging, tracing and debugging

Serveless vs Containers

Both serverless computing and containers enable developers to build applications with far less overhead and more flexibility than applications hosted on traditional servers or virtual machines. Which style of architecture a developer should use depends on the needs of the application, but serverless applications are more scalable and usually more cost-effective. Before we compare serverless computing and containers, let's first discuss containers.A container, according to Docker, is a lightweight, stand-alone, executable package of a piece of software that includes everything needed to run it: code, runtime, system tools, system libraries, and settings.Containers solve the problem of running software when it has been moved from one computing environment by essentially isolating it from its environment. For instance, containers allow you to move software from development to staging and from staging to production, and have it run reliably regardless of the differences of all the environments.Instead of virtualizing the hardware stack as with the virtual machines approach, containers virtualize at the operating system level, with multiple containers running atop the OS kernel directly. This means that containers are far more lightweight: they share the OS kernel, start much faster, and use a fraction of the memory compared to booting an entire OS. There are many container formats available. Docker is a popular, open-source container format that is supported on Google Cloud Platform and by

Google Kubernetes Engine.Developers who choose a serverless architecture will be able to release and iterate new applications quickly, without having to worry about whether or not the application can scale. In addition, if an application does not see consistent traffic or usage, serverless computing will be more cost-efficient than containers, because the code does not need to be constantly running.Containers give developers more control over the environment the application runs in (although this also comes with more maintenance) and the languages and libraries used. Because of this, containers are extremely useful for migrating legacy applications to the cloud, since it is possible to more closely replicate the application's original running environment.It is also possible to use a hybrid architecture, with some serverless functions and some functions deployed in containers. For instance, if an application function requires more memory than allotted by the serverless vendor, if a function is too large, or if certain functions but not others need to be long-running, a hybrid architecture enables developers to reap the benefits of serverless while still using containers for the functions serverless cannot support.

Instead of choosing one or the other, serverless and containers can also be used side by side. Indeed, many companies have found success with a hybrid approach. They:

Use serverless for workloads where serverless meets their needs

Use containers for where it doesn't, for example, for workloads that:

Are long-running

Require more predictable performance

Require more resilience than can be easily achieved with serverless

Run at significant scale constantly, and the pay-per-invocation pricing model becomes too costly

How does serverless computing differ from other virtualization technologies?

VMs, containers and serverless functions have a few fundamental differences. Each approach is defined by the architectural layer that it virtualizes and how compute components are scaled in those respective environments. Hypervisors virtualize the hardware and scale via VMs, while containers virtualize the operating system (OS). Serverless fPaaS virtualizes the runtime and scales via functions, which is why serverless solutions are suitable for projects that have specific characteristics: Runs infrequently; is tied to external events; has highly variable or unknown scaling requirements; has small and short-lived discrete functions; can operate in a stateless manner across invocations; and connects other services together. "Each of these virtualization technologies will be relevant for CIOs in the foreseeable future," says Arun Chandrasekaran, Distinguished VP Analyst at Gartner. "Serverless, specifically, is commonly applied in use cases pertaining to cloud operations, microservices implementations and IoT platforms."

What is FaaS Good at Today?

Having seen all this excitement, let's talk about what is FaaS good at today. The first family of work is embarrassingly parallel tasks. Think about stuff like image and video processing and also, ETL. ETL link data into a storage system. Basically, any tasks that doesn't require coordination, where the requests are usually item potent and the operators are purely functional, where the output purely depends on what data you put into that function.The other family of workload, on the right-hand side, is workflow orchestration. This is an example of workflow from the Autodesk use cases from the Amazon AWS use cases example. There is something like 24 Lambda function invocations was 12 API gateway calls, 8 database accesses, and 7 SNS notifications. The role of Lambda here is to coordinate these tasks. You want to access some database, you want to do some integrity constraint checking, and you want to be able to send the right email to the right user and stuff like that.According to their website, using Lambda actually reduced their user account signup workflow from taking two weeks down to just 10 minutes. I'm not sure like why it takes two weeks in the first place, but obviously, FaaS is pretty good at these types of workload.The issue is that if you go beyond this embarrassingly parallel workload or workflow orchestration stuff, then you're going to hit into some walls pretty quickly, and I'm going to talk about them more in detail soon. In case any of you are from major cloud providers, this is some feedback that we got pretty often when we talk about serverless. We work pretty closely with folks from Google, with folks from AWS, and whenever we talked about serverless, they raise their hand saying, "So I've built this serverless service, and it's called something like Google Cloud Dataflow, or AWS Athena, or Snowflake and so on." I do want to acknowledge that these are all really awesome services. For example, they autoscale pretty well, they take into account data locality, and they do some efficient data movements, all of these good properties that we want, but what we care about is more around generality. We want to be able to enable this general-purpose computing in a serverless mode with all of these nice guarantees that we have. Going back to FaaS, what can't you do on FaaS today? I have here a common list of limitations that we hear folks talk about. The first one is this limited execution lifetime. In Lambda, functions can be 15 minutes long, and in some other cloud providers, it's something like 9 or 10 minutes, so there's this limitation. The second one is no inbound network connection. We can't just open up a port and start sending and receiving messages like what you're used to do when you're deploying a web server, for example.Then IO is a bottleneck. We all know that S3, for example, gives you pretty great bandwidth, but if you're using Lambda, and you want to take advantage of S3's bandwidth, you have to spin up a massive number of Lambda clients, actually tens of thousands of client in order to completely saturate this bandwidth. The problem is, even if you're able to get that bandwidth, latency is usually going to be another issue because if you're doing any sort of data-intensive workload, then the latency from going from Lambda to S3 is usually prohibitive for applications that do require some ultra-low latency.Then finally, there is this no specialized hardware support. If you're doing stuff like computationally intensive training on neural net, or making some prediction using a machine learning models, and you want stuff like GPUs or FPGAs, you're not going to get them currently.In this talk, I'm going to focus on the middle two. The first one, the limited execution lifetime, has been consistently improving over time. When Lambda first launched, it was a one-minute restriction, and then they increased it to five minutes. During last year's reinvent, they further increased it to 15 minutes. We think it's really a configuration thing.The last one, no specialized hardware, we also believe that the cloud providers are probably soon going to address this. We still have this middle two limitations, so no inbound network connections, and IO is a bottleneck.Isn't it just fine? Because everything is functional programming. We can all write Haskell-like programs, it's called AWS Lambda, anyway so you know it must be functional. Functional programming doesn't have any side effects and it's completely stateless. It's not a big deal. The problem is it's not actually the case. As much as the inventor of the Haskell language, Haskell Curry and Simon Peyton Jones might want it to be true, this is not how real applications are built today. I'll talk more about that in a second, but what it really means is that if you're trying to build applications of FaaS infrastructure today, you're not getting Function as a service, but you're actually getting something like dysfunction as a service.The problem is because real applications do share state and they share state in a variety of ways, what it looks like function composition. Say, I have some function G of X that executes and the output has to go as an argument to a second function F. Today, this function chaining phase has to go through a really slow far away storage system like S3. Otherwise, you'll have to play some tax to get it to pass state transparently, which is kind of tough.The second one, another way in which applications share state is via message passing. Say, you work in distributed systems, and you want to build some consensus protocols like Paxos, or you want to build some real-time streaming applications, and you want to play some distributed aggregation techniques to do some analytics. Both of these workloads require low latency message passing. If you don't have inbound network connections, which means that direct messaging is disabled, then you're going to have a hard time building these applications.Then finally, the third one is modifying shared mutable state. Say, you have a database, and you have a bunch of distributed compute agents that want to simultaneously access database, read or write data. Then you have to worry about things like what are the consistency models provided by that database and how do you get performance out of that? All of these things may seem pretty easy, but it turns out that if you try to do them on FaaS infrastructure today, it's all pretty difficult. At the end of the day, FaaS is poorly suited to all of these tasks.

A Platform for Stateful serverless computing

In the spirit of being constructive rather than just complaining stuff, we've been trying to tackle some of these challenges and make serverless computing more general purpose. The direction that we've been headed in is to make state management easier in a serverless context. As the name suggests, instead of pure functional programming, we also want to embrace state. Embracing state is a pretty challenging task, because a successful state management or storage system needs to simultaneously address the issue of high-performance, consistency, and autoscale. Fortunately, we worked exactly on these topics during our PhDs. In the last couple of years, we built a distributed key-value store called Anna that's performing up to 10 times faster than Redis is in certain workloads, and it also quickly adapts to our workload spikes and troughs in a cost-efficient manner. Due to time constraint, I won't be able to go into the technical detail behind

Anna, but if you're interested, please take a look at these two papers listed below, or come talk to me afterwards. The overall message here is that we already have a storage system that can act as a backend for supporting stateful serverless applications.We've been building a system called Fluent right now, which is a fast layer on top of Anna, but obviously this name Fluent collides with the famous Fluentd project so we're trying to come up with a better name here, but for now, we'll just stick with

Fluent. Our design goal is to first keep all the goodies about the current FaaS offering, especially the desegregation of compute and storage, which means that these two tiers can scale independently.FaaS systems like AWS Lambda pioneered this disaggregated architecture, and I want to mention that it's beneficial for a couple of reasons. First of all, from the user's perspective, it reduces costs and enables simple, independent scaling of both tiers, which are great. Also, from the cloud provider's perspective, it actually enables this aggressive bin packing of compute and storage resources, which leads to higher realization, which is one of the holy grails of cloud computing.In addition to all of this, we want to solve all the limitations that we listed previously in order to support stateful serverless application. The key to achieve that is to use Anna for both storage and communication.

What are the advantages of serverless computing?

Lower costs - Serverless computing is generally very cost-effective, as traditional cloud providers of backend services (server allocation) often result in the user paying for unused space or idle CPU time.

Simplified scalability - Developers using serverless architecture don't have to worry about policies to scale up their code. The serverless vendor handles all of the scaling on demand.

Simplified backend code - With FaaS, developers can create simple functions that independently perform a single purpose, like making an API call.

Quicker turnaround - Serverless architecture can significantly cut time to market. Instead of needing a complicated deploy process to roll out bug fixes and new features, developers can add and modify code on a piecemeal basis.

Real-world applications that use serverless computing.

From a programming model perspective, the stateless nature of serverless functions lends themselves to application structure similar to those found in functional reactive programming. This includes applications that exhibit event-driven and flow-like processing patterns.As a comparison, consider an equivalent solution implemented as an application running on a set of provisioned VMs. The logic in the application to generate the thumbnails is relatively straightforward, but the user must manage the VMs, including monitoring traffic loads, auto-scaling the application, and managing failures. There is also a limit to how quickly VMs can be added in response to bursty workloads, forcing the user to forecast workload patterns and pay for pre-provisioned resources. The consequence is there will always be idle resources, and it is impossible to scale down to zero VMs. In addition, there must be a component that monitors for changes to the S3 folder, and dispatch these change events to one of the application instances. This dispatcher itself must be fault-tolerant and auto-scale.Another class of applications that exemplify the use of serverless is composition of a number of APIs, controlling the flow of data between two services, or simplify client-side code that interacts by aggregating API calls.Serverless computing may also turn out to be useful for scientific computing. Having ability to run functions and not worry about scaling and paying only for what is used can be very good for computational experiments. One class of applications that started gaining momentum are compute intensive applications. Early results showthe performance achieved is close to specialized optimized solutions and can be done in an environment that scientists prefer such as Python.If the workloads cannot be easily divided into smaller units (such as Python functions), then batch-oriented systems such as high-performance computing (HPC) or MapReduce clusters are a better option. If the demand for such clusters can be sustained, for example, by having job queues where jobs are submitted and scheduled based on available resources, then workloads can be executed more cheaply, albeit possibly taking longer to complete.

The cost is lower than using FaaS as the service provider can get cheaper VMs either by buying actual servers, using vendor platforms such as Databricks or BigQuery, or getting reserved VMs with longer contracts. If batch workloads can tolerate occasional restarts it may be better to run such workloads with on-demand VMs (such as AWS spot instances).Many "born in cloud" companies build their services to take full advantage of cloud services. Whenever possible they use existing cloud services and built their functionality using serverless computing. Before serverless computing they would need to use virtual machines and create auto-scaling policies. Serverless computing, with its ability to scale to zero and almost infinite on-demand scalability, allows them to focus on putting business functionality in serverless functions instead of becoming experts in low-level cloud infrastructure and server management.

What are functions?

Serverless relies on functions, or more specifically functions-as-a-service, where developers break down their applications into small, stateless chunks, meaning they can execute without any context regarding the underlying server.One of the most popular function-as-a-service offerings is AWS Lambda from the market leading cloud vendor Amazon Web Services (AWS). Launched all the way back in 2014, Lambda allows developers to do just this: run code without provisioning or managing servers. AWS charges you for the compute power you use according to 100 millisecond increments. Developers can therefore focus on their code and event triggers and AWS takes care of the rest.Events could include changes to data in an Amazon S3 bucket or an Amazon DynamoDB table; in response to HTTP requests using Amazon API Gateway; or using API calls made using AWS SDKs. For example, when a user requests a car on a ride sharing app this could trigger the code which is written to fetch a car, or clicking the 'buy' button on an app will trigger that buying process."Lambda is an event-driven execution environment," explains Ian Massingham, chief evangelist at AWS. "So in very simple terms you have code and events, when the event arrives the code is executed for you automatically. So you don't have to pre-position resources or have any standing infrastructure to provide the execution environment."He adds that when the event is triggered, a piece of infrastructure is allocated dynamically to execute the code: "What happens under the covers is a Linux container is started on a machine and details - metadata about the event - is passed into the container at the point of execution."This is opposed to even the 'traditional' deployment model within AWS itself, where "EC2 [Elastic Compute Cloud] instances run web or app servers that wait around for requests and when they come they service them. That gives you floor costs, with Lambda your cost of execution with no traffic is zero and as you start to get traffic you scale up. It is way more cost effective at low levels of usage and way more scalable at high levels of usage, so benefits at both ends of the scale."Massingham says that it is important to note that Lambda doesn't automatically equate to serverless however. "Lambda is the execution part and serverless is a little bit bigger," he says. "Beyond compute you also want to run things like your data stores in a way which doesn't require you to operate infrastructure, a way to do identity management that doesn't require you to operate infrastructure."Amazon CTO Werner Vogels Vogels used an old favourite metaphor during his 2016 keynote: "Before, your servers were like pets. If they became ill you had to nurture them back to health. Then with cloud they were cattle, you put them out to pasture and got yourself a new one. In serverless there is no cattle, only your application. You don't even have to think about nurturing back to health or getting new ones, all the execution is taken care of."

Benefits of serverless computing

From that description, two of the biggest benefits of serverless computing should be clear: developers can focus on the business goals of the code they write, rather than on infrastructural questions; and organizations only pay for the compute resources they actually use in a very granular fashion, rather than buying physical hardware or renting cloud instances that mostly sit idle.As

Bernard Golden points out, that latter point is of particular benefit to event-driven applications. For instance, you might have an application that is idle much of the time but under certain conditions must handle many event requests at once. Or you might have an application that processes data sent from IoT devices with limited or intermittent Internet connectivity. In both cases, the traditional approach would require provisioning a beefy server that could handle peak work capacities—but that server would be underused most of the time. With a serverless architecture, you'd only pay for the server resources you actually use. Serverless computing would also be good for specific kinds of batch processing. One of the canonical examples of a serverless architecture use case is a service that uploads and processes a series of individual image files and sends them along to another part of the application.Improved utilization -- The typical cloud business model, which AWS championed early on, involves leasing either machines --

virtual machines (VMs) or bare-metal servers -- or containers (such as Docker or OCI containers) that are reasonably self-contained entities. Virtually speaking, since they all have network addresses, they may as well be servers. The customer pays for the length of time these servers exist, in addition to the resources they consume. With the Lambda model, what the customer leases is instead a function -- a unit of code that performs a job and yields a result, usually on behalf of some other code (which may be a typical

VM or container, or conceivably a web application). The customer leases that code only for the length of time in which it's "alive" -- just for the small slices of time in which it's operating. AWS charges based on the size of the memory space reserved for the function, for the amount of time that space is active, which it calls "gigabyte-seconds."

No infrastructure management

Using fully managed services enables developers to avoid administrative tasks and focus on core business logic. With a serverless platform, you simply deploy your code, and it runs with high availability.

Dynamic scalability

With serverless computing, the infrastructure dynamically scales up and down within seconds to match the demands of any workload.

Faster time to market

Serverless applications reduce the operations dependencies on each development cycle, increasing development teams' agility to deliver more functionality in less time.

More efficient use of resources

Shifting to serverless technologies helps organizations reduce TCO and reallocate resources to accelerate the pace of innovation.

Separation of powers

One objective of this model is to increase the developer's productivity by taking care of the housekeeping, bootstrapping, and environmental matters (the dependencies) in the background. This way, at least theoretically, the developer is more free to concentrate on the specific function he's trying to provide. This also compels him to think about that function much more objectively, thus producing code in the object-oriented style that the underlying cloud platform will find easier to compartmentalize, subdivide into more discrete functions, and scale up and down.

Improved security

By constraining the developer to using only code constructs that work within the serverless context, it's arguably more likely the developer will produce code that conforms with best practices, and with security and governance protocols.

Time to production

The serverless development model aims to radically reduce the number of steps involved in conceiving, testing, and deploying code, with the aim of moving functionality from the idea stage to the production stage in days rather than months.

Drawbacks of serverless computing

Uncertain service levels

The service level agreements (SLA) that normally characterize public cloud services, have yet to be ironed out for FaaS and serverless. Although other Amazon Compute services have clear and explicit

SLAs, AWS has actually gone so far as to characterize the lack of an SLA for Lambda functions as a feature, or a "freedom." In practice, the performance patterns for FaaS functions are so indeterminate that it's difficult for the company, or its competitors, to decide what's safe for it to promise.

Untested code can be costly

Since customers typically pay by the function invocation (for AWS, the standard arbitrary maximum is

100), it's conceivable that someone else's code, linked to yours by way of an API, may spawn a process where the entire maximum number is invoked in a single cycle, instead of just one.

Monolithic tendency

Lambda and other functions are often brought up in conversation as an example of creating small services, or even microservices, without too much effort expended in learning or knowing what those are. (Think of code that's subdivided into very discrete, separated units, each of which has only one job, and you get the basic idea.) In practice, since each organization tends to deploy all its FaaS functions on one platform, they all naturally share the same context. But this makes it difficult for them to scale up or down as microservices were intended to do. Some developers have taken the unexpected step of melding their FaaS code into a single function, in order to optimize how it runs. Yet that monolithic choice of design actually works against the whole point of the serverless principle: If you were going to go with a single context anyway, you could have built all your code as a single Docker container, and deployed in on Amazon's Elastic Container Service for Kubernetes, or any of its growing multitude of cloud-based containers-as-a-service (CaaS) platforms.

Clash with DevOps

By actively relieving the software developer from responsibility for understanding the requirements of the systems hosting his code, one of the threads necessary to achieve the goals of DevOps -- mutual understanding by developers and operators of each other's needs -- may be severed.

Conclusion

Serverless is a cloud computing execution model where the cloud provider dynamically manages the allocation and provisioning of servers. A serverless application runs in stateless compute containers that are event-triggered, ephemeral (may last for one invocation), and fully managed by the cloud provider.Serverless computing offers several benefits when compared to other computing models, like reduced costs, easier scalability, faster deployment etc. It can also be combined with containers, with some serverless functions and some functions deployed in containers.GlobalDots can help you orchestrate your serverless stack to reduce costs and increase deployment speed.Serverless computing is an evolution in cloud application development, exemplified by the Function-as-a-Service model where users write small functions, which are then managed by the cloud platform. This model has proven useful in a number of application scenarios ranging from event handlers with bursty invocation patterns, to compute-intensive big data analytics. Serverless computing lowers the bar for developers by delegating to the platform provider much of the operational complexity of monitoring and scaling large-scale applications. However, the developer now needs to work around limitations on the stateless nature of their functions, and understand how to map their application's SLAs to those of the serverless platform and other dependent services. While many challenges remain, there have been rapid advances in the tools and programming models offered by industry, academia, and open source projects.